South West Coas

NATIONAL TR

WALKS ALONG THE
SOUTH WEST COAST PATH

Ruth Luckhurst

FALMOUTH TO PENZANCE

COASTAL
PUBLISHING

A Coastal Publishing Limited Book

Editor Alison Moss
Design Jonathan Lewis
Production Peter Sills
South West Coast Path Project Manager Jo Kiddell

First published in 2013 by Coastal Publishing Limited
The Studio
Puddletown Road
Wareham
Dorset BH20 6AE

T: 01929 554195
E: enquiries@coastalpublishing.co.uk
www.coastalpublishing.co.uk

ISBN 978-1-907701-05-4

British Library Cataloguing-in-Publication Data
A catalogue record for this book is available from the British Library.

Printed and bound in Great Britain.

Front cover image: Andrew Ray.

With great thanks to the South West Coast Path Team's partners, who help to maintain and
manage the Coast Path, for providing pictures and contributing to the research for this book.
In particular, we'd like to thank the Cornwall Area of Outstanding Natural Beauty (AONB),
the National Trust and Natural England, as well as all the wonderful photographers who have
supplied their pictures for use in this book.

South West Coast Path

NATIONAL TRAIL

Image Acknowledgements
(key: t:top, m:middle, b:bottom, l:left, r:right, c:centre)
Images in this book are copyright of the photographers and artists.

All Aerial photographs © Coastal Publishing Limited; Front Cover
Andrew Ray; Maria Adlam-Apps 40m; Stephen Bull 5b; Jim
Champion 52t; Simon Cook 58t; S Curtis 48t; Pamela Davies 35,
44b; Julian Elliott 62t; Ted Forman 21t, 58b; Patrick Hanrahan 20t;
Roger Hollingsworth 8t; Ian Killick 62m, 63b; Andrew Lack 41b;
Barry Lockwood 26b, 34m, 48m; Ruth Luckhurst 9t,12t, 13m,
13b, 16t, 17, 26t, 27t, 30t, 30m, 31t, 31m, 45b, 49b, 52m, 53b,
59; Sarah Newby 40t; Jennifer Rowlandson 21m, 45t, 45m; Daniel
Tackley 9b; Bryn Tapper/Cornwall Council 27; Stuart Tormey 34t.

Coastal Publishing Limited and the South West Coast Path Team have made every reasonable
effort to locate, contact and acknowledge copyright owners and wish to be informed by any
copyright owners who are not properly identified and acknowledged so that we may make
any necessary corrections.

CONTENTS

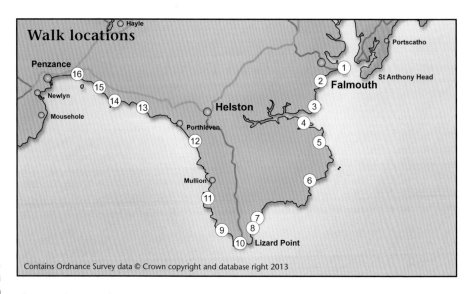

Walk locations

Hayle
Portscatho
Penzance
St Anthony Head
Newlyn
Falmouth
Mousehole
Helston
Porthleven
Mullion
Lizard Point

Contains Ordnance Survey data © Crown copyright and database right 2013

The Lizard peninsula is one of Britain's enduring wildernesses, a remote and rocky finger pointing into the teeth of Atlantic gales and yet warmed enough by the Gulf Stream for sub-tropical plants to flourish in the shelter of its creeks and coves.

Formed from molten rocks thrust from deep within the Earth's crust by enormous pressures some 375 million years ago, it is an area of immense geological importance, as well as great beauty. In its passage to the surface, the embryonic Lizard brought up a slice of rocks in the Earth's crust and mantle, including the green and red serpentine for which the Lizard is famed, and some of these walks visit places where this is spectacularly displayed.

This section of the South West Coast Path passes a major geological boundary where the serpentine gives way to the schists which form the toe of the peninsula. In places these schists have been eroded by sea and weather into dramatic sea caves, such as the Devil's Frying Pan, a chasm 200 feet below the cliffs at Cadgwith,

SAFETY FIRST!
Rockfalls and mudslides are an ever-present hazard on this coast and you are most strongly advised to stay away from the base of the cliffs and the cliff top. See page 64 for more safety information.

where the sea sometimes churns so violently that its central boulder resembles an egg frying.

On both sides of the Lizard, river valleys drowned by rising sea levels after the last Ice Age have formed estuaries providing unique habitats for a wealth of wildlife. In the Helford Estuary more than 80 species of fish flourish, and seahorses and 20 different kinds of sea anemone live in its eelgrass beds. At Loe Bar, tin streaming and mine workings silted up the river, while a shingle bar formed at its mouth from flint moved along the coast from 120 miles east by melting ice, and Loe Pool is one of the county's most popular places for over-wintering birds.

At Marazion Marsh the RSPB Reserve boasts Cornwall's largest reedbed, with more than 250 birds, 500 plants, 500 insects and 18 mammals recorded here, while at Swanpool a nineteenth-century culvert built to lower the water levels in the lake resulted in a brackish lagoon which provided the perfect environment for Britain's only Trembling Sea Mat. The Lizard's biggest wildlife success story, though, is the return of the Cornish chough. Once common enough in Cornwall to become its national emblem, in 1973 the last chough disappeared, and it wasn't until 2002 that a mating pair of choughs flew in and nested in a sea cave. Under the protection of the Cornwall Chough Project 46 choughs fledged in Cornish nests in the next few seasons.

Mining was once an important part of the Lizard economy, producing copper as well as tin, in engine houses like the ones perched dramatically on the edge of the cliff at Wheal Trewavas. Fishing, too, provided a livelihood, and in its heyday Cadgwith boasted a record catch of 1,347,000 pilchards in two days. Capstans and winches, once used to haul in the boats, sit rusting on slipways; while at Prussia Cove you can see the infrastructure of the smuggling activities of the self-styled King of Prussia, a scoundrel with an incongruous reputation for fair play.

Since 350 BC, when trading ships first exported Cornish tin, the waters around the Lizard have been among Britain's busiest, with a third of the world's shipping passing Lizard Point each year. They are also among the most dangerous, and life-saving has always been a pressing concern. In 1752 the lighthouse at the Point was built after heavy losses, and between 1859 and 1961 the lifeboat at Polpeor Cove saved 562 lives.

The geology, the wildlife and the romance of the sea make for wonderful walking all around the Lizard, and the lives of its people over the centuries add a human dimension to its rugged charm.

Public Transport

Falmouth and Penzance are easily reached by public transport, with train and bus links throughout the county.

Most walks give information about the nearest car park. Information about public transport services for these walks can be found online at www.southwestcoastpath.com.

The Traveline South West website provides up-to-date information about all public transport links.
Visit www.travelinesw.com
or call 0871 200 22 33.

INTRODUCTION

Kynance Cove on the Lizard.

Pendennis
Castle

P
Start/Finish

Crab Quay

Pendennis
Point

Falmouth Docks

Walk 1 – Falmouth Docks and Pendennis Castle

Distance	1.5 miles (2.5km)
Estimated time	1 hour
Difficulty	● · · · ·
Ascent	92ft (28m)
Map	OS Explorer Map 103
Starting point	SW 826316

Notes: A tour of some of the historical features of the British Empire's second most important port, with its coastal artillery defences and the famous docks, built after more than 16,000 vessels visited in a nine-year period. An easy, level walk on good paths and pavements.

From the car park on Pendennis Point, pick up the South West Coast Path heading towards the docks, dropping down below Castle Drive to pass the Second World War gun positions at Crab Quay before climbing gently through trees and rejoining the road at Pendennis Rise.

If you wish to visit Pendennis Castle turn left on the road to the Castle entrance opposite. Otherwise turn right and continue along the road to the viewpoint above Falmouth Docks.

Carry on ahead to the T-junction and turn left onto the southern end of Castle Drive and walk back to the car park at the Point. The footpath in the trees on your left en route is a short but pleasant diversion uphill through the woodland if you are feeling energetic.

WALK 1

Pendennis Castle

Coastal defences are thought to have existed at Pendennis since the Iron Age, when a promontory fort was established. There have been suggestions that the Romans also mounted defensive operations.

The blockhouse was built as part of Pendennis Castle, which was constructed between 1540 and 1545, along with St Mawes Castle, across the water. Henry VIII was at war with France and Spain during this time, and the two castles were regarded as a critical link in a chain of coastal artillery fortresses built to defend England from the enemy fleets. Gun ports can still be seen on the lower floor of the blockhouse, and the long platform beside it was used as an artillery site.

In 1598, during the reign of Elizabeth I, a new rampart was built around the castle, and it was strengthened again the following century, prior to the English Civil War. In 1646 the future Charles II hid out here before sailing onwards to the Scilly Isles, and after this the castle was subjected to a further five months of siege before it became the penultimate Royalist garrison on the British mainland to surrender.

Pendennis Point became a focus of resistance to the threat of foreign invasion once again during the nineteenth and twentieth centuries, and it saw significant action during the Second World War. Today the guardroom has been restored to its First World War state.

Crab Quay, just north of the blockhouse, was the best landing place on the headland, and there were guns here by 1700. The two concrete positions visible today were built in 1902 for quick-firing guns used against fast torpedo boats and modified during the Second World War, when they saw considerable action.

Falmouth's famous packet ships arrived at and departed from Custom House Quay, a little way upriver, which from the seventeenth century until 1850 was the only place in Britain where the foreign post came in and out. Bullion was carried, too, on small, fast, two-masted brigs, as well as passengers and some secret government intelligence.

Falmouth Docks

By the middle of the nineteenth century Falmouth had become a major centre of international trade, due largely to the packet's monopoly of foreign communications. It also acquired a certain prestige after Lord Nelson's body was brought home through the port following his victory at the Battle of Trafalgar. In May 1858, a public meeting was held in Falmouth Town Hall, during which it was announced that it had become essential to provide increased accommodation at the port for the loading and unloading, building and repair of the ships visiting the port, by now the second most important in the British Empire. In the previous nine years, the townspeople were told, 16,078 vessels with a combined registered tonnage of over 4,000,000 tons had arrived at the port, excluding coasting vessels, which in themselves were estimated at over 1,000,000 tons.

A committee was appointed to survey the harbour and prepare plans and estimates for dry docks, slips, wharfage and storage accommodation. In November of the same year another public meeting was held to report back on the findings, and in April 1859, an Act of Parliament was passed and Royal Assent received for the formation of the Falmouth Docks and

Engineering Company, charged with the construction of Falmouth Docks.

Between 1860 and 1867, the western wharf and the eastern breakwater were constructed, with the dry dock and gridiron wharf being opened in 1863. The Great Western Railway arrived that year, too, with a line running from Falmouth to Truro, which increased the flow of trade through the port. Shipbuilding began in 1878, and during the early-to-mid twentieth century further wharves were built, while Dry Dock No.2 was enlarged in 1958, being opened by HRH Prince Philip and renamed the Queen Elizabeth Dock.

There is a viewpoint on the pavement above the docks, and a toposcope indicating the layout of the dry docks, wharves and workshops that are spread out below.

Parade of Sail, Pendennis Point.

Rosemerryn
Farm

Tregedna
Farm

Pendra
Loweth

Maenporth

Pennance
Point

Boslowick

Start/Finish

Swanpool

Walk 2 – Swanpool and Maenporth

Distance	4.5 miles (7.35km)
Estimated time	2 hours
Difficulty	●●●●○
Ascent	527ft (161m)
Map	OS Explorer Map 103
Starting point	SW 802313

Notes: An important nature reserve and the home of Britain's only Trembling Sea Mat, Swanpool is an unusual lagoon backed by a rare wooded wetland. With relatively easy ascent and descent, this walk travels on footpaths through a very pastoral area of Falmouth, a world away from its bustling docks and busy streets.

Turn right out of the car park at Swanpool Beach towards Pennance Point and take the first right. Carry on through the woodland bordering Swanpool and turn onto the footpath on your left to carry on through the trees in Swanvale Nature Reserve. Turn left onto the lane leading uphill and follow it up through Boslowick, bearing right at the top and then straight on between the houses to come out on the main road.

Cross the road and pick up the footpath opposite, which will lead to another road. Cross this to follow the footpath opposite, downhill between two fields to come out by Pendra Loweth. Turn left on the road and walk uphill to pick up the public bridleway along the lane on your left. Fork right onto the footpath, around the edges of the fields to Tregedna Farm. This is a working farm: please keep to the path.

WALK 2

Swanpool.

Pass on the far side of the buildings on the bridleway along the drive, turning right onto the lane. Turn left at Rosemerryn Farm on the path to Maenporth. Turn left on the road and walk past the café, picking up the South West Coast Path behind it to return to Swanpool.

A culvert built at Swanpool in 1825 to allow water from the freshwater lake to flow into the sea led to a unique mix of seawater and freshwater, creating one of Britain's most important brackish lagoons. The reduced water level in the lake left an area of marshland to the northwest of it, fed by the six streams winding through on their way to the sea.

This in turn produced a small, densely wooded wetland of mostly willow carr behind the lake – a rare and valuable environment where the willow acts as a filter, removing pollutants before they flow into the lake and providing food and shelter for many birds and small mammals. Willow trees will support as many as 450 different species of invertebrates, which in turn attract a huge variety of birds, and the wet floor and humid atmosphere of this habitat also encourages the growth of rushes, mosses, ferns and lichens.

There is a wealth of bird food on offer in the lake itself: larvae in the mud at the bottom, insects in the reed beds along its shores, and fish and eels which swim through the culvert from the sea.

In all, over 100 different species of birds have been spotted at Swanpool, including mallard, moorhen, coot, little grebe and tufted duck, siskin and kingfisher.

Although the name is probably derived from 'swamp-pool' there are also swans nesting on the lake. However, the black swan which tried to join the lake's community in Spring 2011 caused such uproar among the more peace-loving mute swans that the RSPCA was prevailed upon to remove it to live among its own kind elsewhere.

The species for which Swanpool is famous is underwater and so cannot be seen, but it is the only one of its kind in Britain: the Trembling Sea Mat. This exotic-sounding creature consists of billions of primitive microscopic animals called bryozoa, which live in colonies attached to stones or the stems of plants. Each bryozoan is no more than 2 millimetres in size and is crowned by a ring of tentacles which it uses for filter feeding by catching particles in the water in the hairs on the tentacles.

There is a lane behind the cove at Maenporth called Fine and Brave Lane, allegedly named after the women of Mawnan who acted to protect their community, in the time-honoured tradition of women around the South West coast in times of threats of a French invasion when their men were at sea. Wearing red petticoats they all marched up onto the cliffs, tricking the French into believing that there was a brigade of redcoats ready to defend the coast, so that the enemy turned tail and fled.

Under the cliff are the remains of the Scottish trawler the Ben Asdale, which went aground in a blizzard in 1978.

There are several concrete pillboxes around the cove, sited here in the Second World War to provide cover for this part of the coast.

In the last enemy air raid of the Second World War, a large fuel depot behind Swanpool was blown up. The fuel, planned for use in the D-Day landings, swept through the valley in a massive torrent which threatened the houses below. The flow was diverted, thanks to the prompt actions of US Navy officer Philip Lee Bishop, armed with a bulldozer, and he was awarded the British Empire Medal for his bravery.

Tregedna mouse.

Maenporth.

Mawnan
Smith

Porth
Saxon

Mawnan

Start/Finish

Maenporth

Rosemullion
Head

Walk 3 – Rosemullion Head

Distance	5.25 miles (8.5km)
Estimated time	2½ hours
Difficulty	●●●●●
Ascent	601ft (183m)
Map	OS Explorer Map 103
Starting point	SW 789296

Notes: Starting as a headland walk with wide-ranging coastal views and banks of vivid wildflowers, this route sweeps into the inland waterways of the Helford River, where the Secret Intelligence Service based a flotilla for night-time missions across the Channel to France. None of the ascent or descent is steep, and the paths, though narrow, are along mostly easy terrain.

From the car park at Maenporth, facing inland, turn left up the road to join the South West Coast Path on your left towards Durgan. Stay on the Coast Path until the coastline starts curving around towards Rosemullion Head. Here the left-hand fork takes you around the headland, while the right-hand fork, forking right again, cuts across the headland and joins the Coast Path on the other side.

Continue around the mouth of the Helford River for a little over a mile. Drop downhill past the beach at Porthallack to Porth Saxon. Turn right on the footpath behind the boathouse and follow it uphill through the woods towards Mawnan Smith. Turn right on the lane to join Carwinion Road. Turn left and right onto the small path about 200 yards ahead, through fields to some farm buildings. Taking the footpath to your left before you reach the gate to the road, follow it downhill to the trees at the bottom, turning right in front of the hedge to go into

WALK 3

Durgan.

woodland and climb gently before dropping downhill onto the road at Maenporth. Turn left to return to the car park.

The first written reference to Rosemullion was in 1318, when it was called 'rosemylian'. The name is thought to come from the Cornish word 'melhyonen', meaning 'clover', and as you round the first corner towards the headland in the summer there are swathes of pink clover. The path is a riot of colour at this time of year: purple heather, vetch, wild thyme and thistles, yellow trefoil, buttercups, dandelions and tomentil, blue bugloss and sheep's bit, red campions and speckled white sea campions, white and purple daisies. Carrying on along the path, clumps of montbretia in the gardens bordering the path add to the red of the fuchsias and the pink, white and blue of the hydrangeas, while moths and butterflies flit between them.

When you reach Bream Cove, and Gatamala Cove beyond it, tiny paths lead down to miniature beaches, including Woodlands Beach, part of the National Trust's land at Nansidwell. There are elm trees above the path, and a collection of oaks from all over the world in a little walled garden, as well as an abundance of wild garlic and three-cornered leek in the spring for the wild-food gourmet.

It is thought that there was once an Iron Age cliff castle on Rosemullion Head, defended by a massive rock-cut ditch with a bank some 10 feet higher. Aerial photographs show that there were also two Bronze Age barrows on the site, although there is no trace of them at ground level.

Rosemullion headland was used for defence much more recently, when it hosted a gun emplacement for anti-aircraft guns in the Second World War, although all that remains now are the concrete bases of these and the searchlight emplacements which were part of the station.

Rosemullion Head.

In 1940, the Secret Intelligence Service based its Helford Flotilla at Ridifarne, near Porth Saxon, to maintain clandestine contact with its networks in Brittany. Using traditional Breton fishing boats as well as fast motor launches, the flotilla ran regular night-time missions to remote French beaches, infiltrating agents and collecting airmen. There was a forward base in the Scilly Isles, and operations continued until after D-Day. Many of the troops involved in the D-Day landings left from Trebah, where the concrete jetty remains on what was once a sandy beach.

On the point there is a nineteenth century boundary stone, marking the limits of the Falmouth Borough's area of jurisdiction. This was painted red and renewed every three or four years in a festival known as 'beating the bounds'.

There are two wrecks on the seabed off the headland: the Endeavour, which went down in 1804, and the wooden cargo sloop the Alma, which sank in 1895. Both are below the low water mark and so not visible from the land.

Cornish stiles

Leaving the Coast Path to walk inland, something you soon notice is the Cornish stile. Constructed of granite or slate, depending on the nature of the local rocks, a Cornish stile is usually one of three types: the cattle stile, with a number of long slabs set into the bank of a hedge one above the other like a stepladder; the sheep stile, where a number of square stones are set in a diagonal sequence in a wall to form a set of steps; and the coffen stile (from a Cornish word meaning 'man-made hole'), where several slabs are set like a cattle grid across a trench.

WALK 3

Under Wood

Gillan
Harbour

P

Dennis Head

Walk 4 – Helford, Gillan and Frenchman's Creek

Distance	7 miles (11.25km)
Estimated time	3½ hours
Difficulty	•••••
Ascent	623ft (190m)
Map	OS Explorer Map 103
Starting point	SW 759260

Notes: A figure-of-eight walk that can easily be shortened to a 2-mile (western) or a 5-mile (eastern) loop, this route travels along the remote, romantic Frenchman's Creek of Daphne du Maurier's novel before visiting the tiny beaches of the Helford River and returning through fields and woodland in one of Cornwall's most unspoilt corners.

2-mile loop

From the car park at Helford walk down the road to the river, carrying on past the bridge to bear left on the footpath through the woods, following the KB signs. Fork right towards Frenchman's Creek, going through Kestle Barton and down to the creek, turning right along the riverside path. Fork right uphill, turning right on the track at the top and following the path to Helford via Penarvon Cove.

5-mile loop

Return to the car park and follow the South West Coast Path alongside the Helford River and around Dennis Head. Turn left on the road above Gillan Harbour and follow it towards Manaccan, taking the footpath on the right to follow Vicarage Lane into the village.

Bear right and carry on ahead along the footpath to cross a field to the road. Continue on the footpath opposite to the bottom left of

Gillan Creek.

the field and take the footpath through the trees, forking right and then bearing right through Under Wood to come out on the road above the Helford car park.

The Helford Estuary is a ria, an ancient river valley drowned by rising sea levels after the last Ice Age, 10,000 years ago, and many of the creeks running from it dry to mudflats at low tide. The salt content of the water is high, except after periods of particularly heavy rain, and this makes them an unusually shallow and sheltered habitat for seawater species.

The whole area has recently been formally designated the Fal and Helford Special Area of Conservation (SAC). Identified as being especially noteworthy are the habitats provided by the large shallow inlets and bays, the mudflats and sandflats exposed at low tide, and the sandbanks which are partially covered by seawater at all states of the tide.

No fewer than 80 species of fish have been seen in the estuary, and 20 species of sea anemone in the rock pools along its length.

There are also Biodiversity Action Plans (BAPs) in place here, aimed at protecting the native oyster fishery and the statutory Bass Nursery Area. The Helford is one of the few British locations where the Fan mussel survives, and an important locality for the rare Couch's goby, a small fish that lives in shallow water and is a protected species found only in South Cornwall and Ireland.

As well as the oysters for which the Helford Estuary is famous, sea slugs, cuttlefish and seahorses live in its beds of the rare eelgrass, Britain's only marine flowering plant.

Frenchman's Creek was the setting for Daphne du Maurier's 1941 novel of the same name, featuring the area as it was during the reign of Charles II. The book tells of a rebellious society wife, Dona St Columb, who seeks solitude in her husband's Cornish estate above the creek, after a foolish escapade in London makes her realise the futility of her courtly existence.

Capturing perfectly the sense of the flow of the creeks into the river, where the brown rush of the inland streams whirls leaves and twigs into the tidal wash of the sea, the novel talks of the waders flying low over the mudflats and the gulls wheeling above them, of the call of the curlews and the oystercatchers beneath the trees that crowd thickly to the water's edge from the wooded slopes.

Bluebells near Helford.

The Frenchman of the novel is a pirate, a fellow rebel made cynical by the equally empty lifestyle of the well-heeled courtiers across the Channel, and after one of his men captures Dona in the woods and brings her to his ship moored in a secluded creek, a secret liaison is born between the two. The Frenchman teaches Dona to fish and to cook her catch, and she joins him on a mission aboard La Mouette ('The Seagull'), leaving her children in the care of the nanny and her manservant – who is also the pirate's accomplice – to cover for her absence with a tale of illness.

Looking out to sea from Gillan harbour.

Du Maurier, who lived in the Fowey area after falling in love with it as a child, wrote several novels set in Cornwall, as well as the non-fiction book, Vanishing Cornwall, in which she and her photographer son set about capturing the spirit of a peninsula that she perceived as being about to change forever.

Kestle Barton, on the western loop of the walk and the 'KB' on the signs, is an old Cornish farmstead, some of the buildings dating back to the seventeenth century and built on a site first documented around

1300. The farm is managed within an organic system that also provides a good habitat for wildlife, and the barns have been converted to provide an arts centre. The exhibitions are public and change monthly, and there is a programme of workshops and other events.

Accessed via a path at Penarvon Cove are the wooded slopes of Pengwedhen, donated to the National Trust in 1971 by the daughters of Colonel C.F. Jerram, who 45 years before had been sailing on the Helford River and spotted a 'For Sale' sign. Alarmed at the thought of a housing estate in such a peaceful setting he bought 34 acres, building himself a bungalow in 1926.

Gillan

Treglossick

Porthallow

P

Fletching's
Cove

Nelly's
Cove

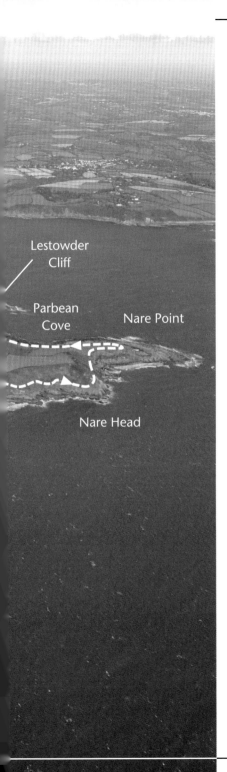

Lestowder
Cliff

Parbean
Cove

Nare Point

Nare Head

Walk 5 – Porthallow and Nare Head

Distance	4 miles (6.5km)
Estimated time	3 hours
Difficulty	●●●●○
Ascent	433ft (132m)
Map	OS Explorer Map 103
Starting point	SW 797231

Notes: Between the fishing village of Porthallow, with its pilchard cellars and net lofts, and the tiny inlet at Gillan, where boats are drawn up on the sand under a fringe of trees, the Coast Path travels through heathland and grassland dotted with wildflowers and astir with butterflies, with tremendous views out to Falmouth Bay. There is some ascent and descent, with steps, but nothing too strenuous.

From the car park at Porthallow take the steps up to the cliff path on your left as you face the sea and follow the South West Coast Path along the edge of the steep slope above Nelly's Cove and Fletching's Cove. Passing Snail's Creep, carry on to Nare Head, dropping downhill past the NCI Observation Station at Nare Point, and round Parbean Cove through a few trees and on along Lestowder Cliff towards Gillan Creek.

Reaching the woodland above Gillan, turn left onto the footpath inland as you reach the beach and follow the lane past the farm to the crossroads. Carry on ahead, turning left to Treglossick and then taking the footpath on the right by the buildings. Cross the footbridge and continue along the valley to Porthallow, turning left on the road and then right, to return to the car park.

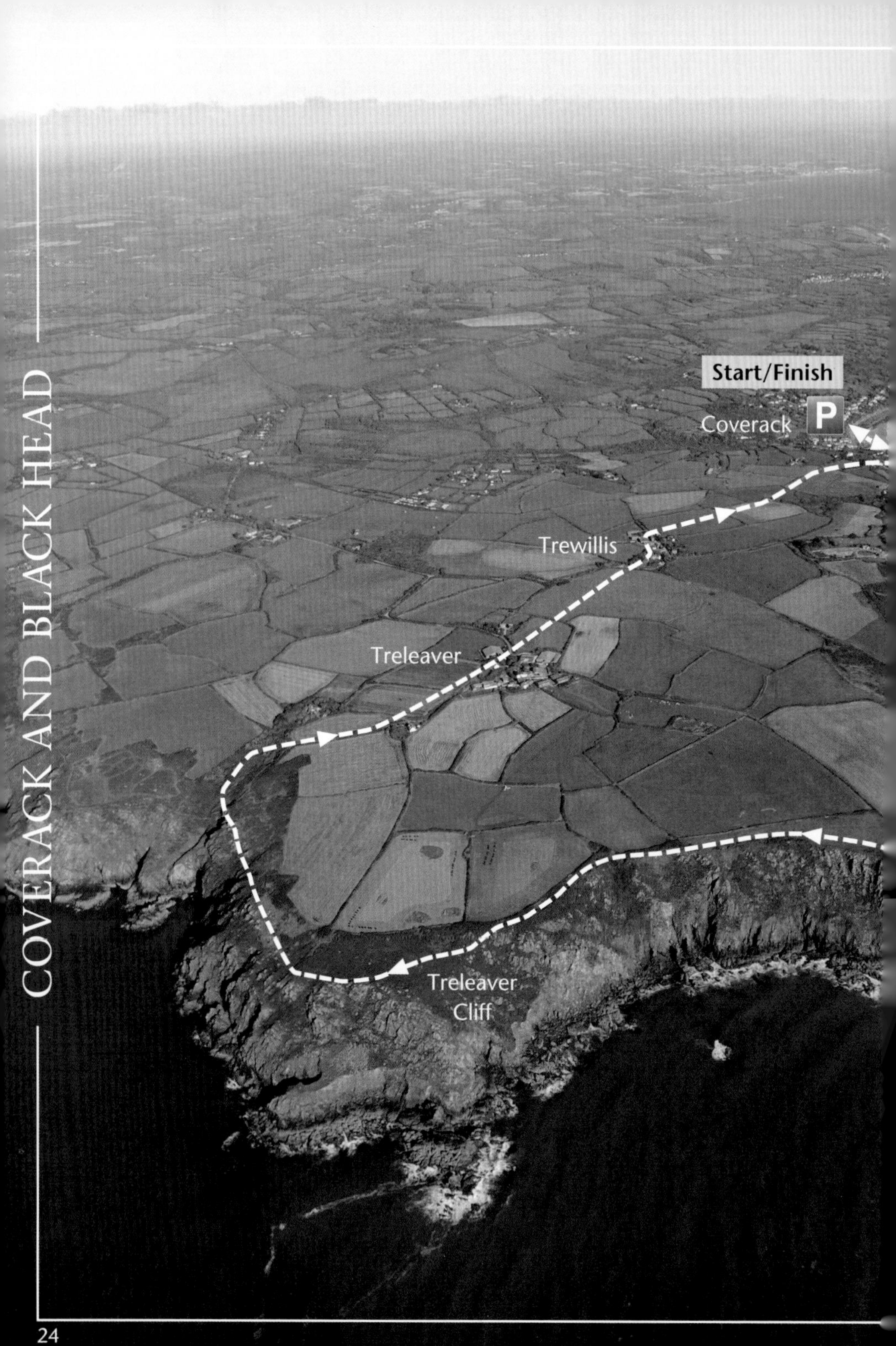

Start/Finish

Coverack

P

Trewillis

Treleaver

Treleaver Cliff

Chynhalls Point

Chynhalls Cliff

Black Head

Walk 6 – Coverack and Black Head

Distance	5 miles (8km)
Estimated time	3 hours
Difficulty	● ● ● ● ○
Ascent	433ft (132m)
Map	OS Explorer Map 103
Starting point	SW 781186

Notes: Starting from the picturesque fishing village of Coverack, an important geological location (see page 31), this walk takes in an Iron Age promontory fort and an optional detour through a sculpture park before travelling through coastal heathland with stunning scenery and returning along footpaths through fields. The path is rocky in places, muddy in others, and there are some steep gradients.

From the car park in Coverack drop down to the seafront and turn right, to walk past the harbour and pick up the South West Coast Path around the headland. Follow it to Chynhalls Point, detouring left here to visit the promontory fort across its tip, and detouring right (uphill) to visit the sculpture park (see page 27). Otherwise, continue along the Coast Path along Chynhalls Cliff to Black Head, around Treleaver Cliff, and turn right onto the track inland before Beagles Point.

Follow the track to Treleaver, picking up the footpath on the right beyond and walking through two fields to Trewillis. Crossing the road here, pick up the footpath opposite around the right-hand edge of the field to the far corner and then take the next footpath right shortly afterwards through more fields to the road. Turn right and drop downhill into Coverack, taking the footpath to the right past the coastguard cottages to return to the harbour.

WALK 6

During the Second World War the docks at Falmouth were a prime target for enemy air raids, and at Nare Point at the southern entrance of Helford Estuary a decoy station was built to draw enemy bombers away from the port. Designed and erected by Ealing Film Studios, the decoy film set featured red and green stop and go lights placed in such a way as to mimic the docks and train depot from a German bomber's cockpit. Remotely controlled from a hidden bunker, sited just off the path in the undergrowth to the left on Lestowder Cliff, the set also simulated shafts of light streaming from an open door and a poorly shaded window. Explosions were also used to imitate trains being bombed. There was a sister site, 14 miles away across Falmouth Bay, at Nare Head.

Helford Passage also played a key part in the Second World War, with a Secret Intelligence Service flotilla running missions between here and the Breton coast (see Walk 3).

Chynhalls Point.

During the Iron Age there was a promontory fort at Chynhalls Point. The remains of the ramparts, defending the point from the mainland while the cliffs gave protection from the sea, have recently been exposed by the National Trust, who have also introduced grazing to control the scrub. As a result, some of the rare and beautiful plants for which the Lizard is renowned are now flourishing, such as Bloody Cranesbill, Camomile, Spring Squill and the spectacular scarlet Thyme Broomrape.

Downas Cove.

Taking the path steeply uphill from Chynhalls Point, and then following the footpath to the left beyond the buildings at the top, will lead you through fields containing steel sculptures by Terence Coventry. Largely depicting birds or people, Coventry's recurring themes here seem to be balance and power. Internationally renowned, with exhibits of his work on every continent, Coventry has a studio nearby.

Coverack Beach is one of only three places in Britain where a fossil Moho can be seen. This is the junction between the Earth's lower crust of gabbro and its upper mantle

Coverack pebbles.

of serpentine, both once molten rock but now cooled and fossilised into the large lumps of rock embedded in the beach. The interpretation board in the car park explains some of the geology; also see Walk 7.

St Keverne and the Cornish Rebellion 1497

St Keverne, near Coverack, achieved national fame as the place where the Cornish Rebellion started in May 1497, and there are bronze statues at the roadside into the village commemorating the event. The rebellion was in response to Henry VII imposing exorbitant taxes to raise funds for skirmishes on the Scottish border, instigated by support from James IV of Scotland for Perkin Warbeck's false claims to the English throne.

Already impoverished, Cornish tin miners were furious with Henry for overturning the historic rights that had been granted them in 1201 by King John, in a charter confirming their 'just and ancient customs and liberties'. These rights protected anyone connected with Cornish tin mining from any jurisdiction other than the Cornish Stannary Parliament in all but the most exceptional circumstances, and a century

later Edward I had exempted Cornwall from all taxes above a certain level.

St Keverne blacksmith, Michael Joseph (known as 'An Gof' – 'the Smith'), took it upon himself to carry his protest to London. At Bodmin, lawyer Thomas Flamank joined him, and by the time they reached Blackheath in southeast London, the Cornish army numbered some 40,000. It was inadequately armed, however, and the rising was easily quelled. The ringleaders of the rebellion were executed, and the others fined.

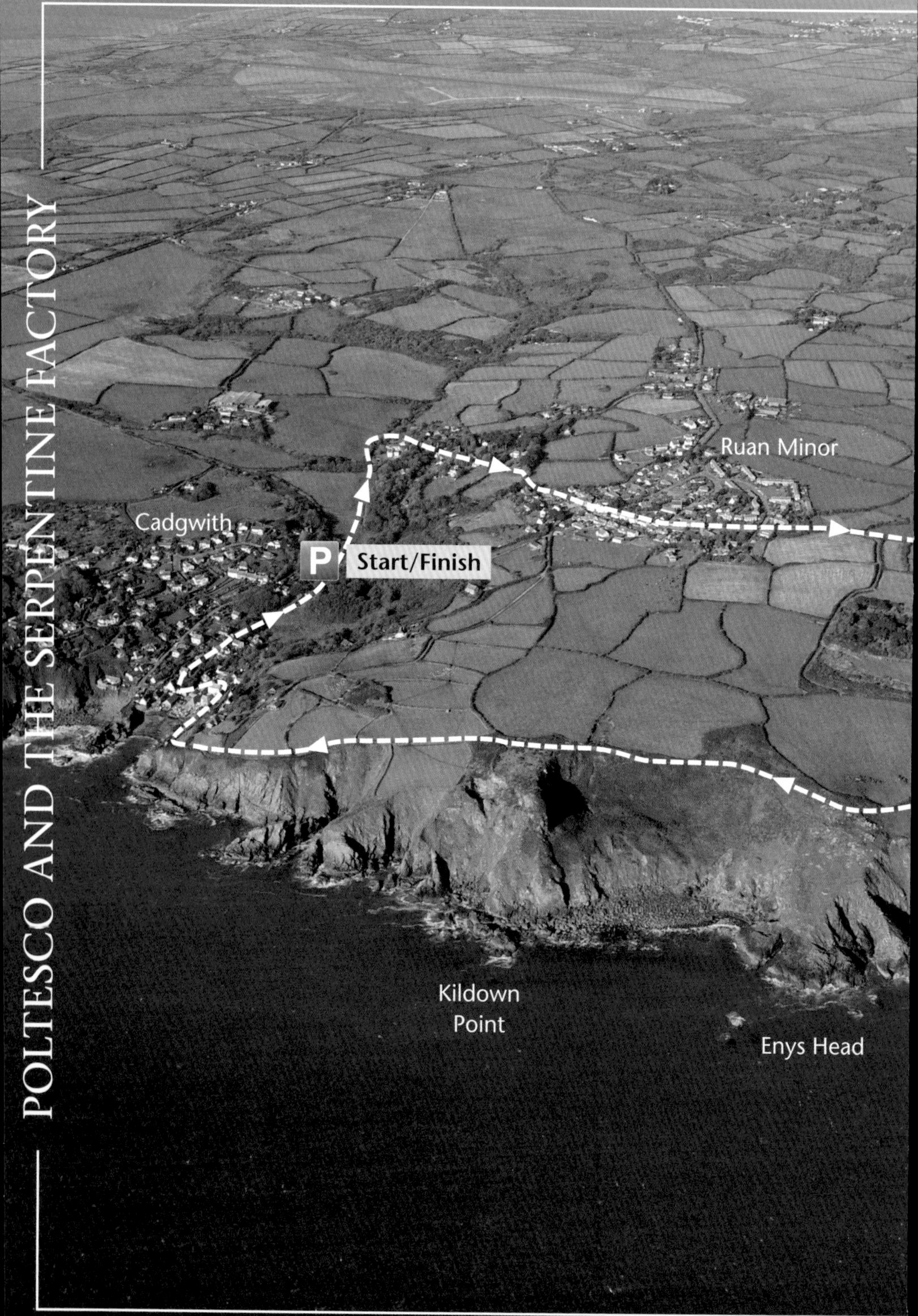

Ruan Minor

Cadgwith

P **Start/Finish**

Kildown
Point

Enys Head

Walk 7 – Poltesco and the Serpentine Factory

Distance	2.75 miles (4.25km)
Estimated time	1½ hours
Difficulty	●● ● ● ●
Ascent	334ft (100m)
Map	OS Explorer Map 103
Starting point	SW 719148

Notes: An easy pastoral stroll from the tiny fishing village of Cadgwith to Poltesco, where an old serpentine factory looks out over the green and pink boulders that line the beach at Carleon Cove, passing a huer's hut where a lookout kept watch for the pilchard shoals that provided the village with its livelihood. There is some ascent and descent, but none of it is too demanding.

From Cadgwith Valley car park take the footpath from the bottom left inland to the road, turning right to pick up the track by the postbox. Fork right and follow the path to Ruan Minor. Turn left by the Spar shop, following the path to the road opposite and crossing it to walk down Poltesco Lane, beside the school, following it all the way to the National Trust buildings at the end. Take the footpath on the right to pick up the South West Coast Path beyond.

Detouring on the tiny path to the left to visit the beach and the old serpentine works, return to continue along the Coast Path to Cadgwith, turning left on Barn Hill and following it around above the beach to turn right onto New Hill and follow it back to the car park.

WALK 7

Kennack Sands south.

POLTESCO AND THE SERPENTINE FACTORY

The collection of buildings by the beach at Poltesco are the remnants of a once-thriving serpentine factory which in the nineteenth century employed 20 men producing polished stone for decorative purposes such as church fonts, shop fronts, mantlepieces and vases. These were ferried by flat-bottomed barges from the quay to waiting ships offshore.

In the original factory there were two machine shops and two buildings used for offices, stores and a showroom, as well as a forge and a three-storey warehouse. The stone was cut, turned and polished by means of a massive water wheel, cast in Helston and measuring 3 feet across, with a diameter of 25 feet. This was turned by water from ponds further up the valley, fed through a leat from a dam across the stream and carried to the factory via a wooden launder high above the wheel.

In 1866 the factory was converted to steam power. A boiler house was added, and a chimney (which has since been

Poltesco Serpentine Factory

demolished), as well as an engine room in the centre of the factory. It is thought that the water wheel continued to provide the power for smaller tasks, while the steam was used for the heavier jobs such as sawing and surfacing.

The factory closed in 1893 and much of it was demolished in the 1930s. The water wheel was converted for chaffing (chopping up straw for animal feed) but was scrapped in 1917, requiring a team of 24 horses to haul it up the cliff track.

The Geology of the Lizard

375 million years ago, at the bottom of an ancient sea known as the Rheic Ocean and located about 30° South of the equator, the molten rock which was to form the Lizard was forced through the Earth's crust, under great pressure, from about 10 kilometres below. The eruptions brought up a complete sequence of the rocks from the mantle to the crust: igneous rocks, volcanic lava and ocean sediments.

Over the next 80 million years the two supercontinents that were separated by the Rheic Ocean began to close the gap between them, powered by plate tectonics. As the landmass of Gondwana (Africa and South America) closed in on Laurasia (Europe and North America), the ocean disappeared and the embryonic Lizard was squeezed upwards and shovelled onto the southern end of what would become Britain.

The collision of the two continents formed part of a single landmass, Pangaea, which subsequently separated, creating a new North America/Asia continent, also known as Laurasia, which travelled northwards for the next 160 million years, towing the Lizard with it. 250 million years ago the Lizard crossed the Equator, less than 100 million years ago it crossed the Tropic of Cancer, and it arrived at its present location just in time for the last Ice Age, when the English Channel flooded and separated Britain from the rest of Europe.

One of the rocks thrust up from beneath the crust, peridotite, was rich in iron and magnesium. As it passed through the

crust and onto what became Cornwall it was changed into serpentine. Mullion cliff (Walk 11) is formed of serpentine, as are the cliffs, stacks and caves at Kynance Cove (Walk 9). Kennack Sands, just north of Poltesco, is a superb place to see some of the other volcanic rocks brought up from deep within the Earth, such as gabbro (top picture) and fossilised lava flows (bottom picture).

Inglewidden

Cadgwith

Devil's Frying Pan

Gwavas Farm

Trethvas Farm

Gwavas
Cliff

P.

Start/Finish

Church Cove

Walk 8 – Church Cove and Cadgwith

Distance	3.25 miles (5km)
Estimated time	1½ hours
Difficulty	●● ● ● ●
Ascent	331ft (101m)
Map	OS Explorer Map 103
Starting point	SW 711126

Notes: A moderately easy walk on the high cliffs above a series of coves and caves. The path crosses an important geological boundary and passes the Devil's Frying Pan, a spectacular hole in the cliffs caused by the collapse of a sea cave. There are metal rings driven into the rocks in places where fishing nets were fastened to haul in the catch. The picturesque fishing village of Cadgwith, with its thatched cottages and stacks of crab creels, boasts of a record catch in 1908, when 1,347,000 pilchards were landed in two days.

From the Landewednack Church car park in Church Cove walk downhill towards the cove to the South West Coast Path. Turn left and climb past a disused serpentine mine and the Balk Beacon to walk along Gwavas Cliff, passing a natural rock arch on your right and an old fisherman's shelter inland. Crossing the stream before Studio Golva turn left for a shortcut (shortens the walk to 2½ miles); otherwise continue past the Devil's Frying Pan towards Cadgwith, bearing right on Prazegooth Lane after the stile.

Turn left and follow New Road out of Cadgwith, turning left after the granite gateposts and carrying on to where a footpath crosses the road. Detour to the right to see the fifteenth-century well then follow the footpath left

Devil's Frying Pan.

through fields past the church. Turn left on the road and left again onto the footpath before the left-hand bend.

At Trethvas Farm take the second path to Landewednack Church and Bass Point. Cross two fields and a stream and climb into an open field to head for the church. Take the track back to the car park.

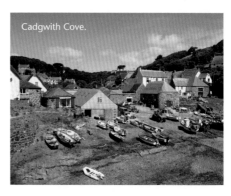

Cadgwith Cove.

The Devil's Frying Pan ('Hugga Dridgee' in Cornish) is a 200-feet-deep chasm above an archway in the cliff to the south of Cadgwith, and it was shown in the 1694 Lanhydrock Atlas. On stormy days the sea washes so violently around the cave that the central boulder is said to resemble an egg frying in a pan. It was formed by the sea eroding a fault in the rock, enlarging it into a cave. As the waves crashed inside they eroded its walls further, while the tremendous pressure caused by the compression of the air inside the cave weakened its roof, which eventually fell in. Ultimately the archway will collapse and a new cove will be formed.

The Balk Beacon is a large red-and-white wooden diamond, mounted at the top of the cliffs at Church Cove. This is a daytime navigation aid, and, used in conjunction with another marker, is used to warn passing ships of the Vrogue Rock below.

The headland at The Balk is a major geological boundary, where the bedrock changes from schist to serpentinite. The rocks around the Lizard Point are schists; that is, rock structures characterised by the parallel arrangements of their constituent materials. From The Balk to the Lizard lighthouse the rock is hornblende schist, with a high content of green and black crystals, while from Polpear to Caerthillian Cove, in the west, it is mica schist, a darker rock banded with silver mica. North of the schists, the central plateau of the Lizard is of serpentine.

The Return of the Chough

Once a common bird in South West England, and especially Cornwall, the last chough disappeared from the county in 1973, following a long decline due to habitat loss and persecution (during the nineteenth and early twentieth centuries many choughs were shot for sport). In 2001, however, four wild choughs were seen on the Lizard, and three took up residence, leading to hopes that they might breed here. The following year two of them began nesting, tucked away in a sea cave, and they became the first choughs to breed in Cornwall (and England) for 50 years. A team of RSPB staff and volunteers set up a round-the-clock watch over the nest to protect the birds from egg collectors, leading to the establishment of the Cornwall Chough Project.

The red-legged, red-beaked crow gets its name from its high-pitched 'chi-ow' call. It has always been an important part of Cornish culture and appears on the county's coat of arms, along with the miner and the fisherman. According to legend, King Arthur was transformed into a chough when he died, and the red feet and beak are said to represent his violent end.

Numbers of choughs had been dwindling throughout Britain since the early nineteenth century, and there are currently only about 300 pairs left, mainly in Wales, the Isle of Man and Western Scotland. Cornwall was their last stronghold in England, but until 2002 the last pair to nest here did so in 1952.

The Cornwall Chough Project was established jointly by English Nature, the RSPB, the National Trust, and the Department for Environment, Food and Rural Affairs (DEFRA). It aims to promote the return of the chough in healthy numbers through encouraging the restoration of suitable feeding habitats by working closely with landowners and reinstating livestock grazing on coastal pastures; monitoring and protecting the birds already in Cornwall; and raising awareness of the wildlife value of well-managed coastal habitats.

WALK 8

Kynance
Cove

Caerthillian
Cove

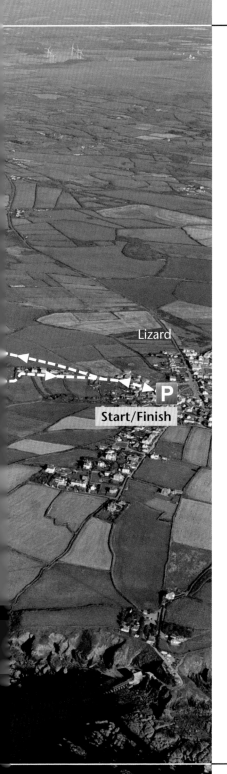

Walk 9 – Kynance Cove

Distance	3 miles (4.75km)
Estimated time	1½ hours
Difficulty	● ● ● ● ●
Ascent	344ft (105m)
Map	OS Explorer Map 103
Starting point	SW 703126

Notes: An easy stroll to one of Britain's most spectacular coves, where Alfred Lord Tennyson wrote of 'the glorious grass-green monsters of waves'.

At the Lizard Green car park take the path past the toilets signed to Kynance Cove, forking right behind the chalet and climbing the steps to walk along the 'double hedge'. At the end carry on through the copse and uphill, to cross two serpentine stiles into a couple of wildflower meadows. Coming to the road to Kynance turn left to the car park.

If you are here at low tide, turn right along the gravel path just before the car park and follow it to Tor Balk for spectacular views across Kynance's south valley before dropping to the north valley through the Cornish heathland of gorse and bell heather. The bushes are alive with robins and blackbirds, dunnocks and wrens, and the little black-headed, chestnut-breasted stonechat scolding from its nest. In spring and autumn look out for ring ouzels, black restarts, whinchats, pied flycatchers and assorted warblers.

At the end of the beach take the steps and then the path back to the car park, and pick up the South West Coast Path on the far side to follow it to Caerthillian Cove. Take the path inland to the left of the stream and rise gently through the valley to fork right and return to The Lizard.

WALK 9

THREE SIDES OF THE LIZARD

Lizard

Start/Finish P

Lizard
Lighthouse

Lizard
Point

Church
Cove

Kilcobben
Cove Lifeboat
Station

Hot
Point

Pyg

Bass
Point

Housel
Bay

Pen
Olver

Walk 10 – Three Sides of the Lizard

Distance	4 miles (6.5km)
Estimated time	2 hours
Difficulty	● ● ● ○ ○
Ascent	620ft (189m)
Map	OS Explorer Map 103
Starting point	SW 703126

Notes: An invigorating jaunt around Britain's most southerly point on the mainland, where the wind is fresh and the rocks offshore are so hazardous that the Admiralty advises navigators to keep a distance of 3 or more miles in rough weather. As a result, much of the history of the Lizard involves shipwrecks and rescue operations.

From the Lizard village green car park walk along Beacon Terrace and on to Church Cove. Turn right onto the South West Coast Path, and climb the steps to follow the cliff tops to the Kilcobben Cove Lifeboat Station. Looking eastwards you can see around the coast to Black Head and on a clear day as far as Prawle Point, the most southerly point in Devon.

Continue past Hot Point and Pyg to the Lookout Station above Bass Point. The white castle-like building is Lloyd's Signal Station, built in 1872 to enable ships entering and leaving the English Channel to semaphore messages to Lloyd's which could then be telegraphed onwards to the ships' owners. Rounding Pen Olver, where you pass two sheds used by Marconi for his early radio experiments, walk around Housel Bay, carrying on past the hotel and on to the Lizard Lighthouse.

Cross the road beyond and continue around Lizard Point, passing the bridleway and two

Frog Rock.

footpaths heading inland. As you gain height at Old Lizard Head, suddenly the view opens up across Mounts Bay to the Land's End peninsula. Turn right onto the next bridleway, marked with blue arrows, and follow it inland along a farm track and back to the village.

The first lighthouse was built at Lizard Point in 1619, but the owners of passing ships were so reluctant to contribute to its upkeep that by 1623 it had fallen into disrepair and was eventually demolished. By 1752 the heavy loss of ships prompted the building of the current lighthouse, which was automated in 1998. It is estimated that a third of the world's shipping passes it each year.

As you head towards the lighthouse, below you to the left is the Lion's Den: a 35-metre deep hole created by the collapse of the roof of a sea cave in 1847.

Lloyds signal station.

The boathouse at the top of the slipway at Church Cove originally housed an auxiliary Lizard Lifeboat; but launching it from the steep slipway was difficult, and in the 14 years it was in operation, from 1885, it was only used twice. At Polpeor Cove, towards the end of the walk, a steep zigzag track descends to the old Lifeboat Station. Between 1859 and 1961 the lifeboat was launched from here 136 times and saved a total of 562 lives.

The Kilcobben Cove Lifeboat Station was opened in 1961 to replace the one at Lizard Point, because the lifeboat can be launched safely from there in virtually all sea conditions. The cliff railway is used to transport heavy supplies and fuel down to the boathouse, and the crew run down the steps to the boat.

The tall wooden post with steps on the side near Old Lizard Head is a wreck post, used to represent the mast of a wrecked ship when lifesaving crews practised rescues with a breeches buoy, a technique used when the sea was too rough to launch a lifeboat and the lifesaving team had to stay on the beach or cliffs. If the shipwreck was near enough to shore, the rescuers used a small cannon to fire a double line and pulley to the ship. The sailors on the ship tied their end of the line to the mast while those on shore attached the other end to a frame anchored in the ground. A harness designed to carry a person – a breeches buoy – was then sent along the rope to the ship, so that those on the sinking ship could climb into the breeches buoy in turn and be pulled to shore.

Close to the Lloyd's building is the National Coastwatch Institute (NCI) lookout post, opened in 1994 after two fishermen drowned within sight of the recently closed Coastguard lookout. There are now 46 NCI stations around the UK coast, equipped and manned by trained volunteers, with further watch stations planned. Most of these NCI stations keep watch over sea, beach and coastline users for over 2,000 hours each year and, like the RNLI, the Institute relies entirely on public donations to continue its lifesaving work.

On 17 March 1907 the 12,000-ton liner SS Suevic struck the Maenheere Reef, off Lizard Point, triggering the biggest rescue in the history of the RNLI. Despite gale-force winds and thick fog, volunteer lifeboat crews from the Lizard, Cadgwith, Coverack and Porthleven rowed out repeatedly, and in 16 hours they rescued all 456 passengers, including 70 babies.

At Pen Olver you pass two sheds used by Guglielmo Marconi in 1900 for his early radio experiments, in conjunction with a much larger station at Poldhu. In January of the following year he set a new record for wireless communication, with a signal transmitted from the Lizard to the Isle of Wight, 186 miles away. In 1902, following further experimental work, he was able to send the first ever transatlantic signals from Poldhu.

WALK 10

Kynance Cove.

Mullion Cove

Lizard National
Nature Reserve

Mên-te-heul

Predannac
Manor Farn

Windyridge
Farm

P

Start/Finish

Predannack
Wollas

Ogo Dour
Cove

Parc Bean
Cove

Walk 11 – Mullion Cove

Distance	3.75 miles (6km)
Estimated time	2 hours
Difficulty	●● ● ○ ○
Ascent	394ft (120m)
Map	OS Explorer Map 103
Starting point	SW 668161

Notes: There is a sense of space and solitude around Predannack Wollas and Mullion Cove, where islands formed by underwater volcanoes are now home to colonies of nesting seabirds and the shoreline has been broken down by weather and the sea into caves and stacks. Although there are some steep ascents and descents, the walk is mostly flat. Here and there the path is muddy, so good footwear is recommended.

From the car park at Predannack Wollas go through the gate past Windyridge Farm, and take the path to the right that leads to the coast. Go over the stile and fork right, turning right along the Coast Path and continuing to Parc Bean Cove and Ogo Dour Cove. From here the terrain is flat all the way around to Mên-te-heul.

Carry on to the harbour before Mullion Cove, turning left on the lane to walk to the road and then turning right on Nansmellyon Road. Take the next road right, forking right again and continuing past three turnings right to take the footpath on the right to the open ground of the Lizard National Nature Reserve. Carry on ahead along this path through fields and along the drive to Predannack Manor Farm.

Continue ahead past the farm, taking the footpath on the left beyond it, through two fields to the road. Turn right to return to the car park.

There are three farms at Predannack, built with local serpentine, with granite quoins (cornerstones) and slated roofs. Two of them belong to the National Trust. These were once part of the medieval manor of Predannack Wollas, which was divided between three tenant farmers Each farm had land of four types: a share in several 'gwel' (or 'gweal'), which were communally-owned arable fields split into strips, or 'stitches', and grazing rights to common land on the outskirts of the 'trev' or cluster of farmsteads; several tiny fields cultivated every year and fertilised with cattle manure; and pastures or crofts beyond the gwel which were ploughed every seven or eight years. As a result of this, the farmland around the trev became very fragmented, as can still be seen today in the number of tiny fields.

A species survey of Lower and Higher Predannack Wollas Farms in 1979 revealed areas of international importance, inland and on the coast. The use of fertilisers was reduced and sprays were amended. Cattle were introduced to graze the area, and Shetland ponies for the more inaccessible areas, with unobtrusive fencing to contain them. This grazing helps to control the scrub and the stronger, taller plants, allowing the lower-growing, less vigorous species to thrive; and as a result there has been a dramatic increase in the number and variety of wildflowers. Noteworthy species include the Powder Blue, ground-hugging Spring Squill, and the wonderfully named Hairy Bird's-Foot Trefoil, prostrate Dyer's Greenweed and Fringed Rupturewort.

The unusual wildlife on the Lizard is due to its unique geology. This is the largest area of serpentine in the country, and in addition, the soil benefits from the deposition of loess or windblown granitic silt, laid down about 16,000 years ago and carried by the wind from glacial deposits on the Irish Sea ice sheet. The warm climate and the salt in the air also contribute their own particular influence to the habitat, giving rise to the right conditions for plants and insects not commonly found elsewhere. Plants that flourish in serpentine include rare sedges

Polurrian Cove

and liverworts, as well as lichens, which thrive on the south-facing slopes. There are also unusual spiders and moths to be found in the maritime heath and grassland.

Mullion's harbour was built in two stages between 1893 and 1895, with the west wall being built first and the south pier added afterwards to enclose a larger area. It was funded by Lord Robartes of Lanhydrock after several disastrous pilchard seasons. The pilchard fishing dried up completely soon afterwards, but the Mullion fishermen were able to build up a lively crab and lobster business instead, selling their catch as far afield as Southampton.

Mullion.

The net store and fish cellars used by the nineteenth-century fishermen can still be seen around the harbour, and the old winch house is still used to haul boats up the slipway, although it uses a modern winch. Mullion Cove continues as a working fishing village, although there are only three boats registered to do so, and the upper storey of the winch house is used to store nets and crab pots.

The Marconi memorial.

The combination of the rocks around Mullion and the westerly gales mean that over time many ships have been wrecked here, and from 1867 to 1909 the Cove had its own lifeboat station. Writing in 1873 the Vicar Of Mullion, the Reverend Harvey, wrote that in just over six years nine ships had been wrecked, 'with a loss of 69 lives, under Mullyon Cliffs, on a bit of coastline not more than a mile and a half in length'.

Facing the prevailing winds as they roar in from the west, Mullion harbour is continually in need of structural repair, and in the last decade of the twentieth century nearly £1 million was spent on this.

Mullion Cove.

LOE BAR

Helston

Lower Nansloe

Penrose Estate

Sycamore Grove

Degibna Wood

Start/Finish

P

The Loe

Loe Bar

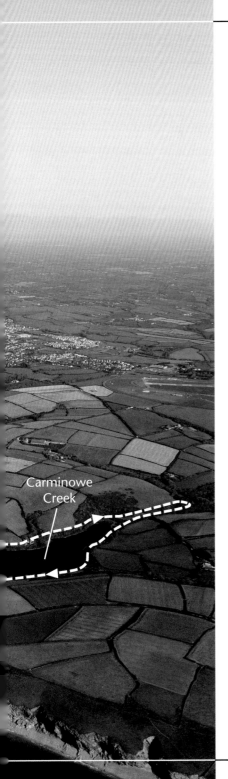

Carminowe
Creek

Walk 12 – Loe Bar

Distance	6.25 miles (10km)
Estimated time	2¾ hours
Difficulty	● ● ● ● ○
Ascent	151ft (46m)
Map	OS Explorer Map 103
Starting point	SW 636248

Notes: A long but flat and fascinating walk around the shores of the lake known as The Loe, taking in a long pebbly beach, where the waves crash deafeningly on the shingle dividing the land from the sea, before continuing through woodland and crossing a massive swamp where cormorants roost in trees rooted in the mudflats. This is where Sir Bedivere is said to have cast Excalibur as King Arthur lay dying.

From the car park in Porthleven (above Parc-an-als cliff) take the South West Coast Path to your left as you face the sea, climbing briefly to walk along the low cliff-tops before dropping to the shores of the lake at Loe Bar. Do not ignore the notices warning of the rip currents and the deep water. Local superstition says that the sea at Loe claims a life every seven years, and the 6-mile stretch of sea from Rill Head to Porthleven is a deadly lee shore that has witnessed many shipwrecks.

Turning left, follow the estate drive along the western shore of the lake through the Penrose Estate. From Penrose Park carry on through Succamore Grove to Helston Lodge, taking the wooden National Trust boardwalk to cross Loe Marsh and the River Cober near the old mine buildings at Lower Nansloe.

Porthleven Harbour.

Turn right down the lane and follow the waymarkers through open fields back to the shores of the lake. Stay by the water through the trees in Degibna Wood and along Carminowe Creek some distance inland before crossing the stream to walk back along the far shore and around to the bar again. Crossing the bar on the shingle is extremely laborious, so take the path along the edge of the grass to retrace your steps along the Coast Path back to Porthleven.

Porthleven.

Local legend has it that the Loe Bar spilt from a bag of sand dropped by the notorious Jan Tregagle, whose ghost roams the county, howling pitifully in the sea caves, in a ceaseless quest to carry out a series of impossible tasks in punishment for his foul deeds as a magistrate in the seventeenth century.

Like the other great bars on the South West Coast the natural shingle dam separating Loe Pool from the sea began to form after the last Ice Age, when the melting ice caused sea levels to rise and push huge amounts of eroded material inland at the mouth of the River Cober, which flows from Helston. The pounding seas of countless winter storms and the longshore drift caused by the relentless wash of undersea currents have continued to shape the bar over the millennia.

Eighty-six per cent of its shingle is flint, and the nearest source of this is around Sidmouth in Devon, 120 miles to the east.

The memorial above the beach at Loe Bar is to the 120 men lost when HMS Anson was wrecked off Loe Bar in 1807. On Christmas Eve the 44-gun frigate left Falmouth to take up position in a navy blockade holding up the French fleet in Brest during the Napoleonic Wars. Gale force winds blew up suddenly, and Captain Charles Lydiard decided to put in and return to Falmouth until they died down.

It proved impossible to do so, however, and three days later the ship was still struggling well leeward of the Lizard. All attempts to clear the land failed and the ship was being forced towards Loe Bar. The captain ordered that the topgallants be lowered and the biggest anchor dropped. The tactic appeared to work and the anchor held, but as the ship pulled around the cable broke, as did the cable on the next anchor dropped. With no other option the captain ordered that the ship should be run full tilt at the shingle bar, in the hope of beaching her in such a way as to minimise the damage.It almost succeeded, but at the last minute the ship broached. Fortunately the mast fell and created a bridge to shore which enabled some of the men to scramble to safety, while others were hauled ashore by villagers who had come down to help in the rescue. Despite this, most of the men were drowned, including the captain, who died trying to save a ship's boy.

As was common practice at the time, the bodies were buried in the cliffs and beaches around the wreck site.

The River Cober flows to Loe Pool from the mining districts Porkellis and Wendron.

From medieval times stream tin was recovered from the valley near Wendron, and for more than 100 years 30 mines operated in the catchment area, resulting in the deposition of mine wastes, including sand, silt and tin slimes, along the river bed and the valley around it. This formed Loe Marsh.

As the sea washed more material onto Loe Bar and its landward side silted up, so it became more impervious to the freshwater. Since this led to flooding in Helston, from time to time the bar was breached to allow the water to flow out to sea. During this period salt water and sea creatures were able to enter the Loe.

The Loe is a Site of Special Scientific Interest (SSSI), chiefly for its bird population, and it is one of the most popular places of refuge for overwintering birds in the county. There is a bird hide on the marsh near Helston, suitable for wheelchair access. Birds most commonly spotted include widgeon, teal, mallard, shoveller, pochard, tufted duck and coot. Of these a few mallard and coot nest here, as well as moorhens and mute swans, and occasionally an unusual migrant such as an osprey is spotted.

Loe Bar memorial.

WALK 12

RINSEY HEAD

Hendra

Praa Sands

Praa Sands

Start/Finish

P

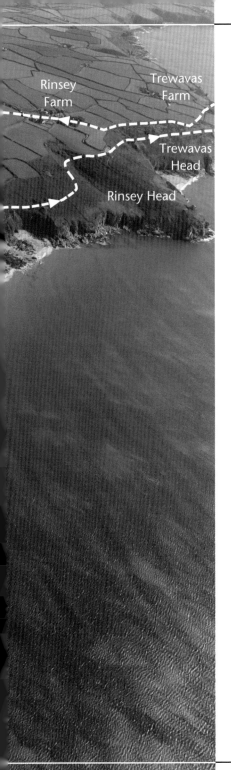

Rinsey Farm

Trewavas Farm

Trewavas Head

Rinsey Head

Walk 13 – Rinsey Head

Distance	3.75 miles (6km)
Estimated time	2 hours
Difficulty	●● ● ● ●
Ascent	402ft (123m)
Map	OS Explorer Map 102
Starting point	SW 576281

Notes: A gentle stroll to an inspiring cove where no fewer than 23 species of butterfly have been seen drifting above spectacular rock formations. Ruined engine houses perch dramatically on the cliffs at Wheal Trewavas and in summer you may spot seals, dolphins and basking sharks in the water below you. Look out for choughs too.

From the bottom of Praa Sands Car Park, pick up the South West Coast Path towards Porthleven and follow it through the dunes and along the drive at Sea Meads to the road at the end. At the end of the houses turn right past the bollards and left of the Coast Path, following it past Lesceave Cliffs to Rinsey Cliff. Cross the track and walk through the National Trust car park to pick up the wide path down to the engine house at Wheal Prosper. Take the path just below the mine to carry on along the Coast Path.

Go over the stile to continue around Trewavas Head, bearing left beyond Camel Rock. Turn left just before Trewavas Mine, inland towards Trewavas Farm. Ignoring the turning to the farm, go over the stile next to the left hand gate. At the end of the field go over the stile and walk alongside the wall above the Coast Path. Keep to the high path, through the kissing gate at the end where it turns abruptly right, and follow it through the buildings to Rinsey Lane. Passing the track

Praa Sands.

to the car park on your left, continue past Rinsey Farm to the two footpaths on the left beyond.

Take the lower path, on the left, through fields to the road from Hendra. Turn left for about 200 yards, forking first right and then left, to take the track above the Coast Path and then the footpath downhill on your left. Turn right at the bottom to return to the Sea Mead drive and retrace your steps to the car park.

St Germoe's Chair.

The odd structure near Wheal Prosper is a bat castle, built on the pile of spoil at the top of Michell's Shaft, the old mine shaft, and designed to prevent people from falling in while allowing bats free access. The shaft is said to plunge 420 feet below the surface, and bats roost in the underground workings as well as in the bat castle itself. If you visit at twilight you will see them flying around the building.

The engine house with its elegant chimney stack was built from slate (or 'killas') from the quarry a little further up the hilllside, and it was strengthened with granite quoins, or cornerstones, with a 30-inch cylinder engine pumping the workings to adit level.

A path near the engine house leads down to Rinsey Cove, if you have time to spare and are feeling adventurous, and at low tide the mine's adit portal can be approached via a cave near the steps at the bottom; but if you do this, take great care. The path down is steep, with loose rocks making it hazardous, and there is a danger of being cut off by the tide.

Despite its name, Wheal Prosper was never particularly prosperous and only traded for six years, closing in 1866. After the building was stabilised by the National Trust it became a popular location for filming, and a television company subsequently reconstructed the mine site to shoot a sequel to Poldark.

Perched perilously on the edge of cliff beyond Rinsey are the engine houses of Wheal Trewavas. These once housed pumping engines for extracting copper from the lodes that extended under the sea here. This is an area of mineralogical importance, and the mine spoil at Trewavas contains sulphides, as well as arsenopyrite, chlorite, mica, pyrite, tristramite, and other minerals.

Rinsey and Trewavas are part of the West Cornwall World Heritage Site. The engine houses at Trewavas have been consolidated by the National Trust, and you can approach them both with care.

Near Rinsey there is a marshy area that attracts birds and butterflies. The mild springs and warm summers in this area allow many wildlife species to flourish, with some unusual visitors often blown off-course by gale-force winds.

The maritime heathland on Rinsey Head consists mostly of gorse, ling, bell heather and tomentil. In late summer, the red stems of the parasitic dodder thread their way through the gorse. Wildflowers found here include rare species like bird's-foot trefoil, and subterranean clover. Wild thyme, sea and musk storksbill, yellow and blue forget-me-nots and common violet also thrive.

The National Trust looks after the land at Lesceave, Rinsey Cliff and Trewavas. Ponies are used to graze the land from time to time, encouraging an abundance of wildflowers which draws many species of butterflies. Look out for the silver-studded blue, the small pearl-bordered fritillary, the green hairstreak, the clouded yellow and the grayling. Butterflies are not the only insects making their home in the cliff vegetation: there are crickets and grasshoppers too, including the great green bush-cricket.

In their turn, the insects attract birds to the heath. Black redstarts live here, as well as wheatears, skylarks and song thrushes. Rinsey Head is also home to one of Cornwall's largest breeding colonies of kittiwakes.

In the churchyard at nearby Germoe, St Germoe's Chair is a small pillared structure with twin arches and a stone bench, and faces carved in the stone. St Germoe was a missionary who arrived on Cornish soil from Ireland in AD 460.

WALK 13

Rinsey Head.

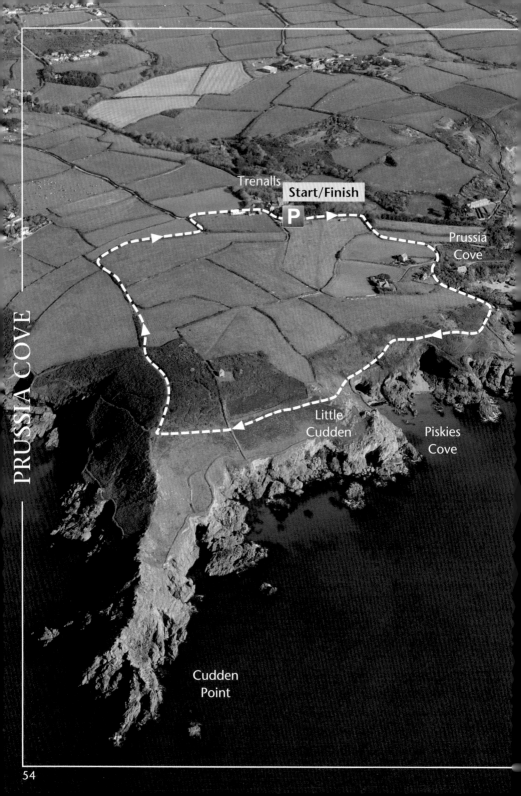

PRUSSIA COVE

Trenalls

Start/Finish

P

Prussia Cove

Little Cudden

Piskies Cove

Cudden Point

Kenneggy
Sands

Bessy's
Cove

Walk 14 – Prussia Cove

Distance	1.5 miles (2.5km)
Estimated time	¾ hour
Difficulty	● ○ ○ ○ ○
Ascent	220ft (67m)
Map	OS Explorer Map 102
Starting point	SW 554281

Notes: A very short walk around the cliffs above the stamping ground of the self-styled 'King of Prussia', an eighteenth-century brigand with a reputation for fairness, who capitalised on the remote and secret nature of the rocky inlets around Prussia Cove to land an enormous quantity of contraband. Be sure to arrive early, because the car park fills up quickly in summer.

From the entrance to the car park at Prussia Cove take the track immediately to the right, and walk downhill past the trees to join the South West Coast Path. Turn right here and follow the Coast Path above the tiny beach at Bessy's Cove. As you progress, you can see the tracks in the rocks where smuggled goods would have been carried up the cliff path to the sheds at the top, and the winch that was probably used for this.

Carrying on around the small point you come to another sheltered inlet at Piskies Cove, with a sandy shore and more caves. Ignoring the path uphill through the heathland continue past Little Cudden and on to the long rocky arm of Cudden Point. (Detour left here for a blast of salty air and terrific Atlantic views.) Take the path uphill to the right at Cudden Point, through the kissing gate and alongside the field edge. Follow the narrow green lane to the road. Turn right to return to the car park.

WALK 14

PERRANUTHNOE

Venton
Farm

Trenow
Farm

Trenow Cove

Walk 15 – Perranuthnoe

Distance	1.25 miles (3.75km)
Estimated time	1 hour
Difficulty	● ○ ○ ○ ○
Ascent	183ft (56m
Map	OS Explorer Map 102
Starting point	SW 539293

Notes: An easy walk on almost level ground, giving tremendous coastal views from Lizard Point to St Michael's Mount, returning along green lanes travelling inland between fields to Perranuthnoe. Unlike the Lizard, the rocks here are soft and crumbling, and the low cliffs are prone to landslides, while the fields are dotted with the disused shafts of copper and silver mines.

At the end of the beach car park at Perranuthnoe cross to the opposite side of the road and go over two stone stiles on to the South West Coast Path. Follow the Coast Path for about a mile, bearing right with it when a small path leads to the beach at Trenow Cove. A little further on, fork right and continue ahead, through the gap in the stone hedge, to the large stone outcrop at Venton Farm, taking the well-worn path that branches to the right and leads inland along the side of the field to a walled green lane. At the waymark post turn right and follow the grass track to Trenow Farm.

Go through a pair of kissing gates and straight across the next field to cross a coffen stile (see Walk 3) and walk uphill past some old mined 'burrows' (waste tips). Follow the farm track past two houses, turning right just after the second to go down a grassy walled lane to Perranuthnoe Church. From here walk through the village to return to the beach car park.

WALK 15

It is thought that Perranuthnoe has been inhabited since prehistoric times. A Bronze Age chambered tomb is suggested by the proximity of a place called Park-an-Chamber, and Roman settlement of the village is indicated by the field names. In the Domesday Book of 1086 it was listed as 'The Manor of Uthno', with a population of eight smallholders, seven villagers and three slaves. Around 1830 its population was over a thousand, thanks to the prosperity of the tin and copper mines, but a century later numbers had dwindled to 742 as the price of tin and copper fell and the mines closed.

Fishermen's huts.

Acton Castle, at Cudden Point, was built by Admiral John Stackhouse, so that he could research the seaweeds growing there. A slipway was built to enable him to bring seaweed up from Stackhouse Cove (later named after him), and a seawater bath was cut in the rock beside it for his wife to bathe. He was a noted authority on seaweeds, and a genus – the Stackhousia – was named after him.

Prussia Cove was originally named Porthleah but renamed after its most famous smuggler, John Carter, who called himself the King of Prussia.

John Carter and his two brothers, Harry and Charles, ran a very lucrative contraband business, using the inlets at Piskies Cove and Bessy's Cove as well as Porthleah for their exploits. The natural seclusion of Porthleah, as well as the shape of the cliffs above, made this the perfect landing place for an illegitimate cargo, and the many caves in the rock were ideal for its storage.

Despite the illegal nature of his trade, however, John Carter was scrupulously

Prussia Cove.

fair-minded. After customs officers confiscated a cargo of tea, Carter broke into their stores at the dead of night and reclaimed his goods – but he didn't touch a single item that he didn't consider to be rightfully his. (It seems that the customs men knew from this just exactly who had plundered their stores, such was his reputation for straight dealing!)

Praa Sands is an important area for its geological features. These include the granite cliffs at Rinsey Head, as well as the fossilised peat bed that is visible as a black platform beneath the dunes near the café. Analysis of pollen samples from the peat have shown that alders grew nearby: evidence that this was a forest before it was submerged by rising sea levels after the last Ice Age.

At the base of the cliffs at Sydney Cove is a red-brown ridge of rock protruding into the sea, formed 270 million years ago, when molten rock deep in the Earth's crust pushed its way through a vertical crack to form an elvan dyke. If you take a closer look, you'll see that the feldspar crystals in it are all lined up in the same direction.

Copper Mining

The mineral wealth of the district made it a highly profitable place for mining, and in the 1850s and 60s there were numerous mines around Kenneggy.

At the height of production in the 1850s, Cornwall produced about 80 per cent of Britain's copper and was said to be the world's most important copper-mining region. However, new mines being constructed in North and South America were able to produce the metal at a much lower cost, since they didn't need the extensive pumping required by the wet Cornish mines, and when the value of ore slumped dramatically as a result, many of the local mines slowed production and even stopped operating altogether. A further slump in the value of lead, zinc and tin in the 1860s compounded the situation.

Wheal Grylls, on Greenberry Downs, however, was working on a rich vein of tin that provided some protection against this downturn in fortune. The Great Western Mine sett (the ground

granted to a company of miners, of which it was a part), reached its peak in 1871, when it was producing something like £10,000 of tin a year.

Following further extensive prospecting in the early part of the twentieth century, a plant and mill were built and an underground venture set up at Wheal Boxer, but hopes proved to be unfounded and before long this mine closed too.

Start/Finish

P

Penzance

Longrock

St Michael's Mount

Marazion

Walk 16 – Penzance and Marazion

Distance	3.25 miles (5km)
Estimated time	1½ hours
Difficulty	●● ○ ○ ○
Ascent	79ft (24m)
Map	OS Explorer Map 102
Starting point	SW 476304

Notes: As easy saunter along the shoreline to Marazion, linked by causeway to St Michael's Mount. Catch the bus back to Penzance, or follow the waymarkers for St Michael's Way to return inland via Marazion Marsh, an RSPB Reserve which is particularly popular with over-wintering birds.

From the sea wall in the main car park in Penzance head towards the station, and pick up the South West Coast Path beyond. Follow it alongside the sea wall to the far end of the beach, by the café, continuing along the beach and then the dunes and into Marazion. Regular buses travel into Penzance from The Square in Marazion; or walk back along West End and then Green Lane, forking left after the caravan park to pick up St Michael's Way across the RSPB Reserve at Marazion Marsh to return inland via Eglos. (For details of this inland return route see the South West Coast Path website).

Marazion is one of Britain's oldest towns, having received a royal charter from Henry III in 1257, and it was the area's main town until late medieval times, when Penzance took over the role. It is also known as 'Market Jew'; but the name has nothing to do with any Jewish community that might have settled here. Like

St Michael's Mount.

the main street in Penzance, which shares the name, it is derived from the Cornish 'Marghas Yow', meaning 'Thursday Market'.

As well as the Thursday market, traditionally Marazion had another important market known as 'Marghas Byghan', or 'Small Market'. In medieval times markets and fairs were important trade events, and the first recorded fair in Marazion was in 1070, just four years after the Norman Conquest and 16 years before the famous Domesday Book compiled the details of every settlement in the land.

Tide covering the causeway.

St Michael's Mount was a busy maritime centre as long ago as 350 BC, when trading ships exported Cornish tin to other European countries. In AD 495, the Archangel St Michael is said to have appeared to some fishermen on the island, and within a few years it had become a thriving religious centre.

After the Norman invasion of 1066 it was granted to the French Benedictine abbey

of Mont St Michel. The chapel on its summit was built in 1135 by the French abbot Bernard le Bec and was dedicated to St Michael, who was the patron saint of high places, as well as being a dragon slayer (the dragon in question being the old pagan religion).

In 1193 the island was seized by Henry le Pomeray on behalf of the Earl of Cornwall (later King John), who disguised his men as pilgrims. After four miracles allegedly took place on St Michael's Mount in 1262–63 it became a major pilgrimage destination, but throughout the next few centuries it saw its share of action of a less contemplative nature. In 1473 the Earl of Oxford held it under siege for six months during the War of the Roses, while in 1549 Cornish rebels in the Prayer Book Rebellion were more successful and managed to seize it after Henry VIII pensioned off its clergy as part of his Dissolution of the Monasteries.

In 1588 the first Armada beacon was lit here, warning of the presence of the Spanish fleet in the English Channel; and during the English Civil War, it was a Royalist stronghold between 1642 and 1646. After it was surrendered to the Parliamentarians, Colonel John St Aubyn was appointed Governor of the island and shortly afterwards bought it from the Bassett family. The St Aubyn family continued to own it until Francis St Aubyn gave it to the National Trust in 1954.

According to local mythology, a giant by the name of Cormoran once lived on St Michael's Mount and waded ashore periodically to steal cows and sheep. A local boy called Jack rowed out to the island one night and dug a deep pit while the giant slept. Stumbling downhill the next morning, Cormoran was blinded by the light of the rising sun and fell into the pit and perished.

The RSPB Reserve at Marazion Marsh boasts Cornwall's largest reedbed, and more than 250 birds, 500 plants, 500 insects and 18 mammals have been recorded here.

Species to look out for on the reserve are cetti's warbler, chiffchaff, grey heron and little egret, while in the summer damselflies and dragonflies flit around the yellow flag and green phragmites reeds. Bitterns are regular winter visitors and some years starlings roost here between October and December, their dazzling aerobatic displays attracting buzzards and sparrowhawks. It is also a stop-off point for many migrating species, with birds heading south in search of warmth for the winter and other flocks arriving from the north.

The reserve is open all the time and entry is free, although donations are always welcomed by the RSPB. Dogs should be kept under control and should not be allowed into open water.

St Michael's Mount

Covering 630 miles from Poole to Minehead, the South West Coast Path National Trail leads you through diverse landscapes, all with their own unique story to tell. If the walks in this book have inspired you to find out more about the longest and most popular of the UK's 15 national trails, visit www.southwestcoastpath.com.

Natural England – www.naturalengland.org.uk
Natural England is the government's adviser on the natural environment and provides the majority of the funding for the maintenance of the Coast Path, which is undertaken on a day-to-day basis by Devon County Council and the National Trust. Through Environmental Stewardship Schemes, Natural England also helps farmers and other landowners to protect and enhance the countryside so that nature can thrive.

National Trust – www.nationaltrust.org.uk
The National Trust Countryside Team works seven days a week to restore and care for the characteristic wildlife of the area, as well as working with local communities to improve access and understanding of these special areas. Regular events and opportunities to get involved mean that all ages can help shape their countryside.

South West Coast Path Association – www.southwestcoastpath.org.uk
If you enjoyed these walks, why not join the South West Coast Path Association? This charity represents the users of the trail, campaigns to improve the path and raises money to help it happen. By joining you'll be one of thousands who help to make the South West Coast Path one of the world's greatest walks.

Cornwall Area of Outstanding Natural Beauty – www.cornwall-aonb.gov.uk
The Cornwall AONB makes up approximately a third of the county and is in 12 separate parts. The landscape is diverse and ever changing, cherished by those whose families have worked in it for generations and loved by those who are seeing its beauty and mystery for the first time. It is the essence of Cornwall.

SAFETY
On the beach and coast path

- Stay away from the base of the cliffs and the cliff top and ensure that children and dogs are kept under control.
- Do not climb the cliffs. Rockfalls can happen at any time.
- Beware of mudslides, especially during or after wet weather.
- Always aim to be on the beaches on a falling tide and beware of the incoming tide, especially around headlands. Be sure to check the tide tables.
- Beware of large waves in rough weather, especially on steeply shelving beaches.
- Observe all permanent and temporary warning signs; they advise on hazards and dangers. Check routes beforehand by visiting www.southwestcoastpath.com

- Be very careful on rocky foreshores which often have slippery boulders.
- Stay within your fitness level – some stretches of coast can be strenuous and/or remote.
- Make sure you have the right equipment for the conditions, such as good boots, waterproof clothing and sun screen if appropriate.
- Follow The Countryside Code.

Emergencies
In an emergency dial 999 or 112 and ask for the Coastguard, but be aware that mobile phone coverage in some areas is very limited.